MAR - - 2023

STARK LIBRARY

CINQUAIN POEMS

By Ruthie Van Oosbree Poems by Lauren Kukla

Big Buddy Books

An Imprint of Abdo Publishing
abdobooks.com

abdobooks.com

Published by Abdo Publishing, a division of ABDO, PO Box 398166, Minneapolis, Minnesota 55439. Copyright © 2023 by Abdo Consulting Group, Inc. International copyrights reserved in all countries. No part of this book may be reproduced in any form without written permission from the publisher. Big Buddy Books™ is a trademark and logo of Abdo Publishing.

Printed in the United States of America, North Mankato, Minnesota
052022
092022

Design: Emily O'Malley, Mighty Media, Inc.
Production: Mighty Media, Inc.
Editor: Jessica Rusick
Cover Photograph: FatCamera/iStockphoto
Interior Photographs: alexei_tm/Shutterstock Images, p. 17; Alpha Stock/Alamy Photo, p. 5; Aquarius Studio/Shutterstock Images, p. 23; Brothers91/iStockphoto, p. 11; Catrin1309/Shutterstock Images, pp. 24, 25 (star); Gabriele Rohde/Shutterstock Images, p. 13; grey_and/Shutterstock Images, p. 7; Igor Dutina/iStockphoto, p. 6; insemar/iStockphoto, p. 21 (child); Jihan Nafiaa Zahri/Shutterstock Images, p. 27 (girl); Marti Bug Catcher/Shutterstock Images, pp. 14–15 (rocky stream); Monkey Business Images/Shutterstock Images, p. 9; Nestor Rizhniak/Shutterstock Images, p. 29; Oleksandr Khoma/Shutterstock Images, p. 15 (river); Pixel-Shot/Shutterstock Images, p. 25 (girls); sabelskaya/iStockphoto, p. 21 (dolphin); Smit/Shutterstock Images, p. 19; Waerabkk/Shutterstock Images, p. 27 (diaper); ZHUKO/Shutterstock Images, p. 18
Design Elements: mhatzapa/Shutterstock Images (paper doodles); Mighty Media, Inc. (backgrounds)

Library of Congress Control Number: 2021953299

Publisher's Cataloging-in-Publication Data
Names: Van Oosbree, Ruthie; Kukla, Lauren, authors.
Title: Cinquain poems / by Ruthie Van Oosbree and Lauren Kukla
Description: Minneapolis, Minnesota : Abdo Publishing, 2023 | Series: Poetry power | Includes online resources and index.
Identifiers: ISBN 9781532198922 (lib. bdg.) | ISBN 9781098272852 (ebook)
Subjects: LCSH: Poetry--Juvenile literature. | Poetry and children--Juvenile literature. | Cinquains, American--Juvenile literature. | Rhyme--Juvenile literature.
Classification: DDC 821.0--dc23

CONTENTS

Cinquains 4
Fitting the Form 8
Nature Cinquains 12
Animal Cinquains 16
Sports Cinquains 20
Friendship Cinquains 22
Gross Cinquains 26
Sharing Your Cinquain 28
Glossary 30
Online Resources 31
Index 32

CINQUAINS

Cinquains are five-line poems. There are many types. One is the American cinquain. It was created by poet Adelaide Crapsey. Crapsey's cinquains often described a single subject or idea. They also used few words.

TIPS & TRICKS
"Cinquain" is pronounced *SIN-cane.*

Kids usually write **didactic** cinquains. A didactic cinquain is a simpler form of the American cinquain. The lines describe the first word of the poem. Each line contains different types of words.

Watermelon

Juicy, sweet

Dripping, slurping, smacking

So messy to eat

Yummy

—Anonymous

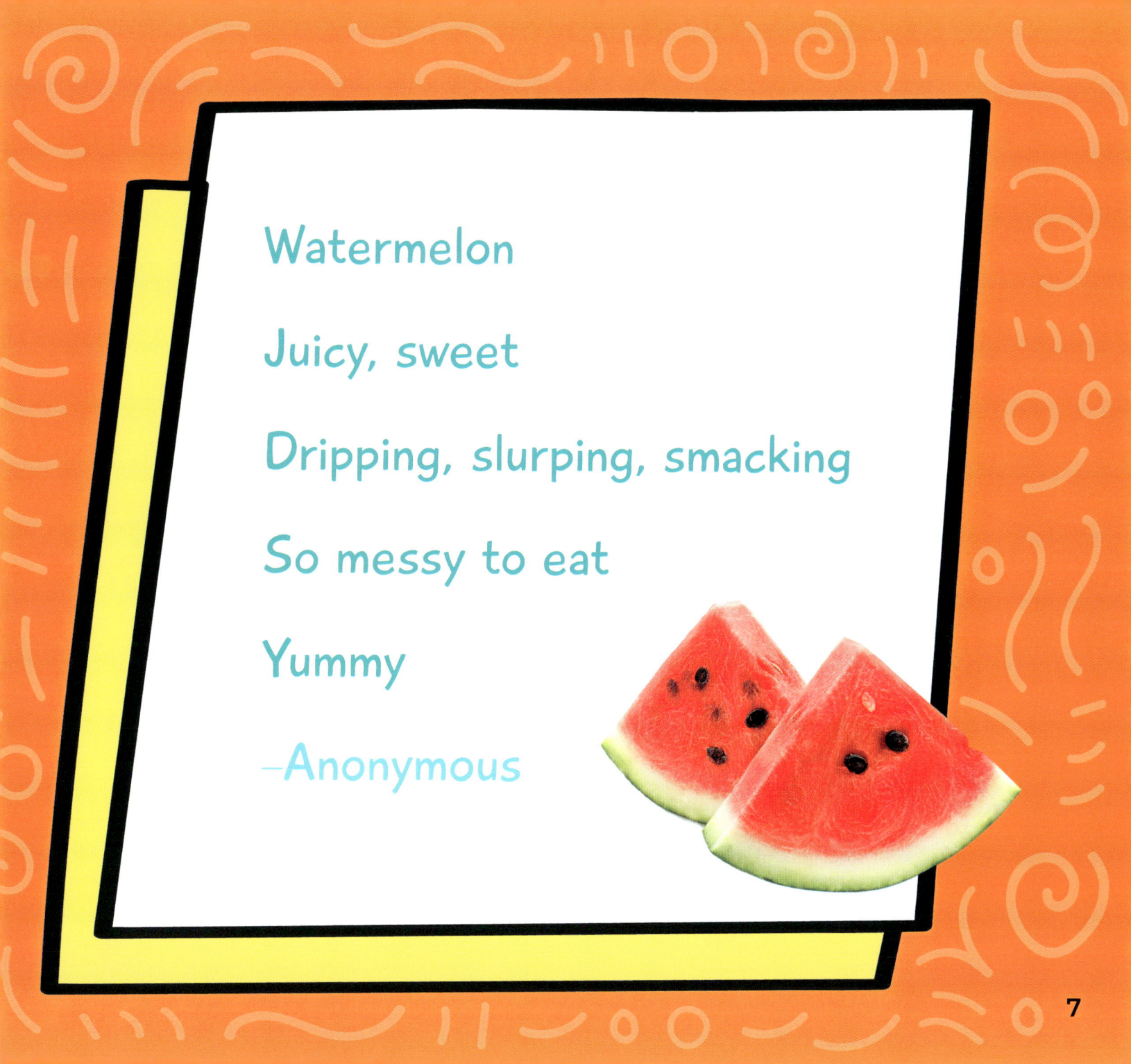

FITTING THE FORM

To write a cinquain, first choose a **noun** to be your subject. This is the first line. The next line is two **adjectives** describing your subject.

The third line contains three words that show action. They should describe things the subject does.

Many action words end in -ing. Examples include running, jumping, and climbing.

The fourth line is four words long. It is a **phrase** that adds more detail about the subject.

The last line of a cinquain is one word. The word should be related to the subject. It is often a **synonym** or descriptive word.

NATURE CINQUAINS

Many cinquains are about nature. Before beginning your poem, spend time outside. Pick a subject that inspires strong feelings. Write down **adjectives** about your subject. How does it look or sound? Use these words in your poem.

TIPS & TRICKS
Cinquain topics can be general (water) or specific (pond).

A nature cinquain can also be about a season, such as autumn.

Next, list action words. You might describe the subject as if it were a person. This is called **personification**. What does the subject make you think about? This could be your four-word **phrase**. Does the subject remind you of something? This word can end the poem.

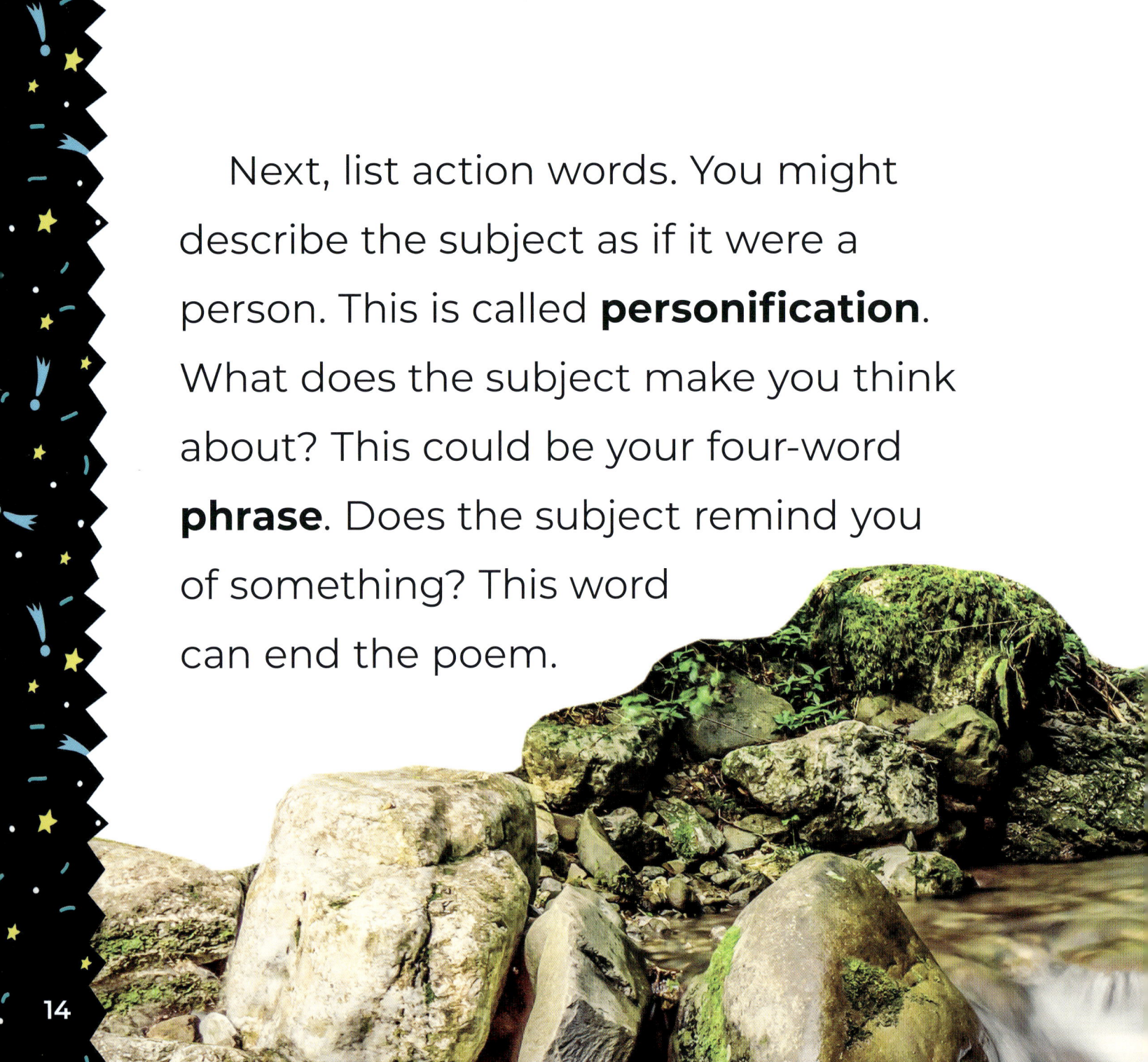

Creek

Little, rocky

Laughing, tumbling, playful

Cool feet, warm heart

Refreshing

ANIMAL CINQUAINS

Animals make great cinquain subjects. It is often easy to come up with action words for living things. Choose a favorite wild animal or pet. Write down words describing how the animal moves and acts. Use these words in your poem.

Try including a pet's favorite activities in your poem.

The animal's **physical traits** can also inspire your poem. Traits could include fur color or body shape. Think about things that set the animal apart. Write four-word **phrases** about a few of these traits. Use one in your cinquain.

Pete

Dark green

Swimming, hiding, sleeping

Hard shell, soft inside

Turtle

SPORTS CINQUAINS

There are many ways to write a sports cinquain. Describe what it's like to play your favorite sport. Or write about the sport's star athlete. You could even write about a piece of sports **equipment**. Describe what happens to the equipment during a game.

Swimming

Graceful, speedy

Splashing, kicking, paddling

Spinning like a dolphin

Racing

FRIENDSHIP CINQUAINS

Write a cinquain about a friend or family member. His or her name can be the first line. **Adjectives** can describe the person's **personality**.

Choose action words for things he or she does often, like *laughing*.

Get creative with your four-word **phrase**. You could describe how you met a friend. Or say how that person makes you feel.

The last line could be a friend's nickname. Or name an object or animal your friend reminds you of.

○ ○ ○ ○ ○ ○ ○ ○ ○ ○

Sister

Annoying, fun

Joking, caring, playing

Here for me always

Friend

GROSS CINQUAINS

Pick a gross subject for your cinquain. This might be an object, smell, or creature. Choose words that are just as gross as your subject. Describe how the subject oozes, stinks, or slithers!

TIPS & TRICKS

Choose your words carefully. Think of your cinquain as a small story!

Diaper

Dirty, forgotten

Hiding, rotting, reeking

Growing stinky, stinkier, stinkiest

Disgusting

SHARING YOUR CINQUAIN

Cinquains can be shared in many ways. You can read your poem out loud to friends. You might ask a parent's permission to post it online. Or write your cinquain on a poster. Draw a picture to go with it!

Try posting your poem on a poetry-sharing website.

GLOSSARY

adjective—a word that describes something.

didactic—used to teach people something.

equipment—items needed for a certain activity.

noun—a word referring to a person, place, or thing.

personality (puhr-suh-NA-luh-tee)—the set of emotions and behaviors that make some people different from others.

personification—describing an object or animal as though it has human-like abilities.

phrase—a brief expression containing two or more words.

physical—able to be seen and touched.

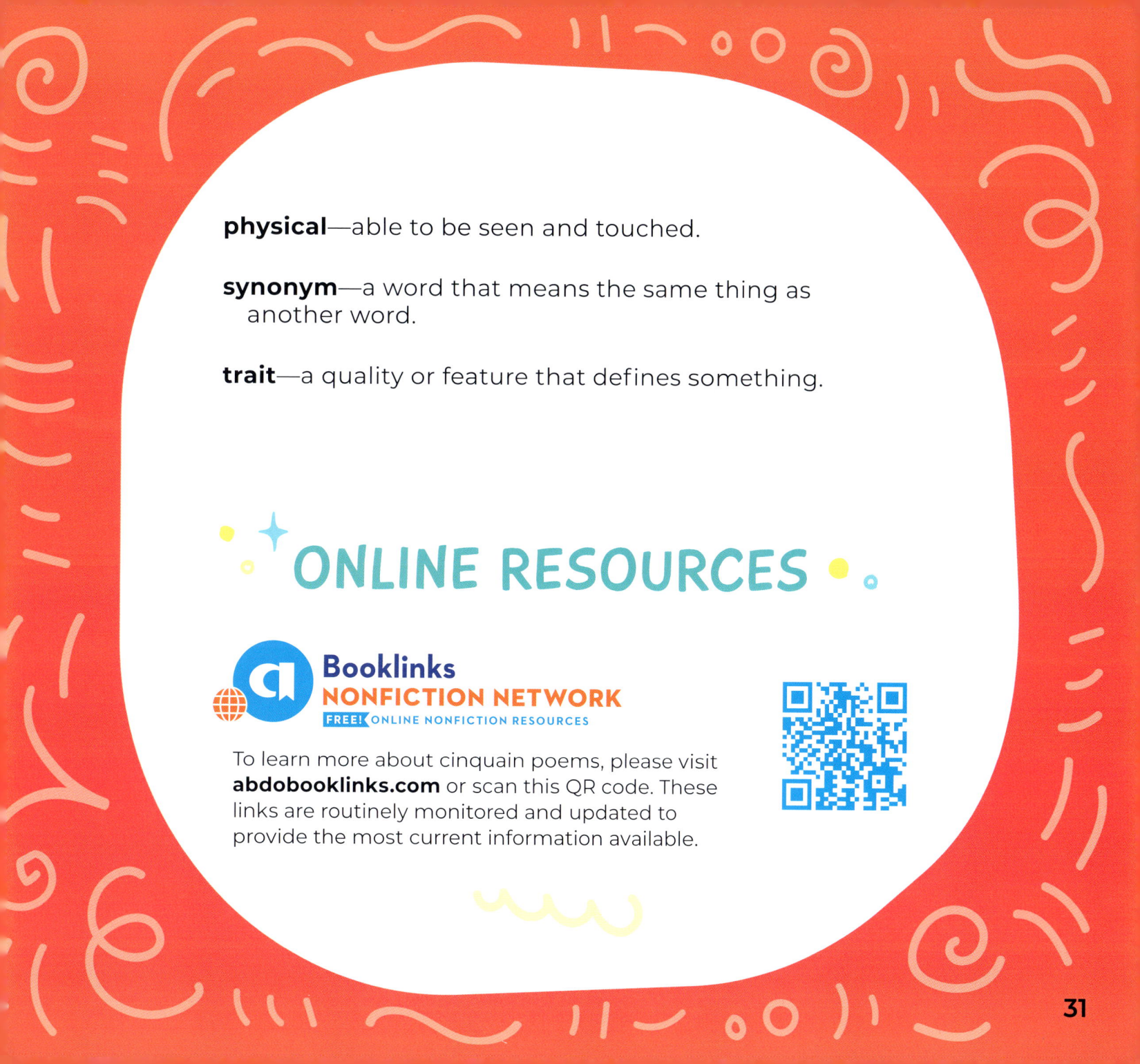

synonym—a word that means the same thing as another word.

trait—a quality or feature that defines something.

ONLINE RESOURCES

To learn more about cinquain poems, please visit **abdobooklinks.com** or scan this QR code. These links are routinely monitored and updated to provide the most current information available.

INDEX

action words, 8, 9, 14, 16, 22

adjectives, 8, 12, 22

American cinquain, 4, 6

animals, 16, 17, 18, 19, 21, 24

Crapsey, Adelaide, 4, 5, 6

feelings, 12, 24

friendship, 22, 23, 24, 25, 28

gross things, 26, 27

lines, 4, 6, 8, 10, 22, 24

nature, 12, 13, 14, 15, 16, 19, 21

nouns, 8

personification, 14

sharing, 23, 28, 29

sports, 20, 21

3 1333 05237 4509